Hants & Dorset Recollected

The final 20 years

Looking back at the last two decades before Hants & Dorset was broken up in 1983

Chris Harris

First published in 2021

British Library Cataloguing in Publication Data

A catalogue record for this book is available from the British Library.

ISBN 978 1 85794 578 2

Silver Link Books
Mortons Media Group Limited
Media Centre
Morton Way
Horncastle
LN9 6JR
Tel/Fax: 01507 529535

email: sohara@mortons.co.uk
Website: www.nostalgiacollection.com

Printed and bound in the Czech Republic

Contents

Frontispiece: **POOLE BUS STATION** This photograph was taken during the days leading up to Christmas 1975 – a Christmas greeting can be seen on the wall of the Sports Centre in the background. A mixture of Bristol LH, RE, FS, FLF and VRT buses can be seen together with a Leyland Atlantean that Hants & Dorset had acquired with the Winchester-based King Alfred fleet in 1973 and subsequently transferred to Poole. By this time considerable progress had been made in repainting the Hants & Dorset fleet into National Bus Company poppy red, although, as can be seen, a few vehicles remained in the traditional green livery. *Hants & Dorset*

About the author

Chris Harris spent his career in the bus industry. He joined Hants & Dorset Motor Services as a conductor at Poole depot back in the days when that company's buses were painted in Tilling green livery. After some years on the road, Chris was seconded to the Market Analysis Project in 1978, and later worked in Hants & Dorset's publicity department until the company was broken up in 1983. He then joined the Wilts & Dorset Bus Company, becoming Marketing Assistant in 1986 and Head of Marketing in 1993.

Chris remained in that role when the Go-Ahead Group bought Wilts & Dorset in 2003, and subsequently became Public Relations Manager for the Go South Coast family of companies in 2007, a position he held until his retirement a few years ago.

In retirement Chris has edited the Go South Coast staff magazine and also edits *Wessex Review* magazine for the Wessex Transport Society. He has also written a number of books on transport and local history, while also finding time to enjoy classical music and reading.

Dedication

Very sadly Brian Jackson passed away while this book was being prepared for publication. The book is dedicated to his memory.

HANTS & DORSET

Introduction

In 2016 we celebrated the centenary of Hants & Dorset buses when the company, if not the name, was 100 years old at that time. As part of these celebrations *The NOSTALGIA Collection* published my book *Hants & Dorset Recollections*, which told the story of the hundred years from 1916 to 2016, showing how Bournemouth & District and subsequently Hants & Dorset had developed into the Morebus and Bluestar operations, which provide such an excellent service for local people in the 21st century.

Hants & Dorset Recollections sold rapidly and has been out of print for some time. Now, in 2021, it was considered that it was time for another book about Hants & Dorset, this time concentrating on the final 20 years that the name was used on the sides of buses – i.e. 1963 until 1983. By great good fortune I became aware of an extensive stock of photographs taken by Neil Goodrich, the majority of which had not previously been published, and Neil has been kind enough to allow them to be used as the mainstay of this book. Neil's photographs were mostly taken in two batches – when he was a teenager during the late 1960s and when he was working for Hants & Dorset during the late 1970s – so they have been combined with some other photographs taken during the 1960s, 1970s and early 1980s to provide an illustrated history of the final years of Hants & Dorset Motor Services before the company was broken up into smaller operating units in April 1983. I have been fortunate enough to have been able to use photographs taken by Phil Davies, Brian Jackson and the late Harold Stevens in addition to those supplied by Neil Goodrich. Brian Jackson has also provided valuable technical support, which has been very much appreciated. To all of these people, together with Peter Townsend and staff at

The NOSTALGIA *Collection*, I offer my warm thanks; it would have been impossible to have produced this book without their help.

As we look at the changes that took place at Hants & Dorset during the 20 years from 1963 to 1983, it is also opportune to look back at the changes that took place in our day-to-day lives during that period. In many ways 1963 was something of a watershed year in British social history. It was the year in which the so-called 'Swinging Sixties' really got under way and many previously entrenched attitudes were reconsidered. The year began with record low temperatures and heavy snowfalls that remained until early March. Then on 27 March came the publication of the Beeching Report, which in due course was to lead to significant railway closures, including some in the Hants & Dorset area. On the popular music scene groups were starting to dominate the charts – the Beatles, for example, had three No 1 hits during the year.

There were certainly many significant happenings in the 20 years between 1963 and 1983. In 1963 television had consisted of just two channels, BBC and ITV. BBC2 started in 1964, while 1967 saw the introduction of Radio 1, and the existing Light Programme, Third Network and Home Service were rebranded as Radio 2, Radio 3 and Radio 4 respectively. British Railways finally phased out the use of steam locomotives in 1968, and it was also during that year that the postal system was divided into 1st and 2nd class. The big event of 1969 was the first landing of a man on the moon by the USA.

In 1970 the age of majority in the UK was reduced from 21 to 18, while 1971 brought the introduction of decimal currency. The school leaving age was raised from 15 to 16 in 1972, and

restrictions on broadcasting hours were lifted, allowing the growth of daytime television. The UK joined the Common Market (EEC) in 1973, and New Year's Day became a public holiday in England for the first time in 1974. The year 1976 will be remembered for the exceptionally warm, dry summer. We celebrated the Silver Jubilee of Her Majesty the Queen in 1977, while the later months of 1978 saw an increase in strike action that was to lead in early 1979 to serious disruption across the country, exacerbated by very cold weather, which gave rise to the headline 'Winter of Discontent'.

Something of a sea change in politics saw the election of Margaret Thatcher as Prime Minister in May 1979, and perhaps a sign of things to come was the deregulation of express coach services in 1980. Argentina invaded the Falkland Islands in 1982, precipitating the Falklands War. Channel 4 television started broadcasting in 1982, while 1983 saw the introduction of the pound coin and the start of breakfast television.

Returning to the bus industry, it was from 1 January 1963, and under the provisions of the 1962 Transport Act, that the British Transport Commission was abolished and replaced by various separate boards to control the nationalised transport sector. The state-owned bus companies, including Hants & Dorset, became the responsibility of the newly created Transport Holding Company. This was the start of a number of changes that in due course would have significant effects on Hants & Dorset and its customers. Please join me as we remember the final 20 years, 1963 to 1983, of Hants & Dorset buses.

Chris Harris
Poole, Dorset.

The green bus years

BOURNEMOUTH BUS STATION

This photograph was taken on a summer day in 1963. Open-top Bristol K5G, fleet number 1143, registration number GLJ 986, can be seen in the foreground, with a good load of passengers for Swanage. However, the rear destination blind does not tell the full story. The open-top bus will, in fact, only run as far as Sandbanks Ferry, where the passengers will alight and go as pedestrians over the ferry to catch two waiting single-deck buses at Shell Bay for their onward journey to Studland and Swanage. There were, it is true, regular through buses between Bournemouth and Swanage, but only single-deck buses could use the ferry at that time, and these had insufficient capacity for the summer. However, the enjoyment of an open-top bus trip on a pleasant day, followed by the ferry trip, more than made up for the fact that the bus did not go directly through to Swanage.

The bus itself is of considerable interest. GLJ 986 had been new to Hants & Dorset in February 1948, carrying a standard 55-seat Eastern Coach Works lowbridge body. In June 1957 this body had been replaced by the 59-seat highbridge open-top body seen here, which had been built in Hants & Dorset's own bodyshop in May 1953, and which from 1953 until 1957 had been carried by an older vehicle in the Hants & Dorset fleet. The cream-liveried open-top buses were known affectionately by the crews as 'banana boats', and were very popular with passengers on the Sandbanks routes during the 1960s; GLJ 986 was in service with Hants & Dorset until 1970.

Another similar open-top bus can be seen among the parked vehicles on the right, and to the right of it is one of the batch of six AEC Regent III double-deck buses with 53-seat lowbridge bodies by Northern Counties that were diverted from Western SMT in Scotland to Hants & Dorset when new in 1949. This vehicle is easily distinguished from the other parked buses by the two smaller windows in the upper deck rear emergency door. The summer of 1963 was the last chance to see any of these AEC Regent double-decks in service, as the entire batch was withdrawn in September of that year.

Other buses in the photograph include Bristol K and LD double-decks and a Bristol L single-deck – just as would be expected at that time.
The late H. Stevens, courtesy of Julia Stevens

WEST OVERCLIFF DRIVE, BOURNEMOUTH Hants & Dorset operated an extensive range of coach touring holidays, and also day excursions by coach, during the 1960s. Bristol MW6G 2693 RU was delivered new to Hants & Dorset in April 1963, carrying an Eastern Coach Works body with comfortable fixed seats for 39 passengers; coaches used on holiday tours were fitted with 30 reclining seats to provide extra space and legroom for travellers. 2693 RU was posed for this photograph on West Overcliff Drive shortly after delivery to Hants & Dorset. Subsequently it remained in the coach fleet long enough to be painted in National white livery with a red waistband in March 1973, then in National Bus Company dual-purpose livery (red below the windows and white above) in June 1974. *The late H. Stevens, courtesy of Julia Stevens*

WEST OVERCLIFF DRIVE, BOURNEMOUTH Bristol MW6G 1472 LJ had been new to Hants & Dorset in June 1961 and illustrates the earlier style of coach body that was fitted by Eastern Coach Works. On entry into service this coach had 30 reclining seats for holiday tours, but when photographed in the spring of 1963 it was being used to advertise Hants & Dorset's coach touring holidays. Holidays advertised in the 1963 brochure included five days visiting the Norfolk Broads and East Coast for 20 guineas (£21.00), four days to Devon Cornwall & the Isles of Scilly for 16gns (£16.80) and 15 days to the Scottish Highlands and John O'Groats for 55gns (£57.75). The brochure pointed out that 'The best possible hotels and restaurants are used, and these are regularly inspected. The coaches are especially designed for long-distance observation touring, with adjustable armchair seats spaced so as to give ample leg room.' 1472 LJ was in the Hants & Dorset coach fleet until 1969, when it was converted to a 37-seat driver-only-operated bus, in which guise it remained in service until 1976.
The late H. Stevens, courtesy of Julia Stevens

Left: **BOURNEMOUTH BUS STATION** During the years following the end of the Second World War a large number of lowbridge-bodied Bristol Ks joined the Hants & Dorset fleet. The AEC-engine K6As were especially associated with Hants & Dorset's Western Area, and they were a common sight at Bournemouth depot and also on some of the longer services at Poole depot until the mid-1960s. On a particularly inclement day in March 1965 Bristol K6A HRU 855 is seen awaiting its next call to duty. The bus looks a little travel-weary following quite an eventful life. When new in April 1949 it was diverted to London Transport to help with a serious shortage of buses in and around the capital, and did not start work with Hants & Dorset until April 1950. It continued in service with Hants & Dorset until April 1967. *Phil Davies*

Below left: **GROSVENOR SQUARE, SOUTHAMPTON** The 70-seat rear-entrance Bristol FL was quite a rare variant – only 45 were produced out of a total of 5,218 Bristol/Eastern Coach Works Lodekkas that entered service across the country between 1953 and 1968. Hants & Dorset had 12 of the 45 FLs built, and they had entered service in two groups of six in November 1961 and December 1962. The first of the December 1962 batch, 7682 LJ, is caught by the camera at Grosvenor Square, Southampton, in July 1967. Notice the additional short window bay on both decks. The aluminium rear wheel discs were carried by this vehicle from 1964 until later in 1967. *Phil Davies*

Right: **STANDEE** single-deck buses were an innovation that was imposed on Hants & Dorset's customers at the beginning of 1967. They were also the first buses to be bought new by Hants & Dorset since 1950 that were not of Bristol/Eastern Coach Works manufacture. The first of the standee buses to be built was HRU 695E; this Bedford VAM14 had a Strachan body with a front entrance and centre exit, and was able to carry 33 seated passengers together with a further 25 standing. The single forward-facing seats can be seen in the rear section behind the centre exit door. This photograph was almost certainly taken for Hants & Dorset before the bus was exhibited on the Strachan stand at the Commercial Motor Show in September 1966; it was delivered to Hants & Dorset in December of that year and entered service in January 1967. Another four similar buses were taken into stock between February and May 1967. Standee single-deck buses were understandably less than popular with the travelling public, and all five were rebuilt to a more conventional layout with 41 seats (plus 19 standing) between February 1968 and September 1969. *The late C. J. Burt collection*

Left: **BOURNEMOUTH BUS STATION** A very large private hire was clearly being undertaken when these coaches were photographed during the summer of 1968. From 1964 onwards the managements of Hants & Dorset and the Salisbury-based Wilts & Dorset had started to merge, and it can be seen that at least five Wilts & Dorset vehicles and drivers have been called upon to take part in the operation seen here. Closest to the camera we see (left to right) 1473 LJ, a Bristol MW6G new to Hants & Dorset in June 1961; HAM 503E, a Bedford VAM14 from the Wilts & Dorset fleet, new in 1967; and 2693 RU (see page 5). *The late H. Stevens, courtesy of Julia Stevens*

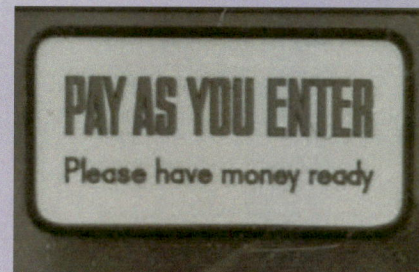

PAY AS YOU ENTER

Please have money ready

WARSASH The Hants & Dorset route 78 ran between Woolston and Warsash via Bursledon and Park Gate. Taken in December 1968, this photograph shows Bristol LD6G SRU 994, which had been new to Hants & Dorset in January 1957, laying over at the Warsash terminal point, awaiting time to return to Woolston. Note the traditional concrete and asbestos bus shelter together with the old-style bus stop flag. Notice also the fine array of British cars that can be seen. By the 1960s bus services were becoming less remunerative, and – like many other companies – Hants & Dorset had to look for economies. One of the more significant savings came from the extension of driver-only operation instead of having a crew of driver and conductor on most buses. This had been the case for years on some of the quiet rural routes, but driver-only operation started to become more widespread from the late 1960s onwards. This photograph shows one of the last crew-worked journeys on route 78 before it was converted to driver-only operation. *Phil Davies*

NORTH STREET, POOLE The first Hants & Dorset bus garage in Poole had been a relatively small building by the George Hotel in Wimborne Road, which still stands but has not been used for transport purposes for many years. A garage in Towngate Street, the northlight roof of which can be seen in the left background of this picture, was opened in January 1932, and by the 1960s buses were parked on land between the garage building and North Street, as seen in this photograph, taken in July 1968. The double-deck bus closest to the camera, JEL 275, is a lowbridge-bodied Bristol K5G that was in service with Hants & Dorset from 1950 until 1969. The destination blind is marked up for route 25, which at that time ran between Wimborne and Blandford via Tarrant Keyneston; it is likely that JEL 275 had operated a short journey between Wimborne and Shapwick. Also in the photograph are a pair of Bristol MW saloons – former coaches that have now been converted for bus work – and a couple of Bristol Lodekkas. This area of Poole has changed so much that not a single building illustrated here survives in the 21st century. *Phil Davies*

WOOLSTON Delivered new in December 1968, NLJ 817G was Hants & Dorset's first Bristol LH6L and entered service on Sunday 5 January 1969 on route 78 between Woolston and Warsash; this photograph was taken at Woolston after it had operated its first journey on the – from then – driver-only-operated route. Notice the very shallow windscreen; NLJ 817G was subsequently rebuilt in May 1974 with a taller front windscreen, reducing the depth of the dome containing the destination blind. *Phil Davies*

ALMER Following the four Strachan-bodied Bedfords that entered service in 1967 (see page 7) together with one example bodied by Willowbrook, Hants & Dorset bought ten more Bedford single-deck buses, which were delivered during May/June 1968. This time they were the Bedford VAM70 model and the dual-doorway bodywork by Willowbrook had conventional-style seating for 40 passengers. MRU 70F is seen at Almer in March 1969; at that time route 29 ran one round trip on Thursdays and Saturdays only – 13.30 Bere Regis to Blandford, arriving at 14.09, and returning from Blandford to Bere Regis at 15.30 (Thursdays) or 16.15 (Saturdays). Notice the beautiful and historic St Mary's Church in the background. *Phil Davies*

Above: **BLOXWORTH** Through the 1960s and most of the 1970s Hants & Dorset's routes 90 and 91 ran between Poole and Bere Regis via Lytchett Matravers and Morden, then either via Winterborne Kingston (route 90) or Bloxworth (route 91). Given the rural nature of the routes, quite a good level of service was provided, making it possible for villagers to work office hours or shop in Poole. Bristol FS6G ALJ 574B, which had been new in July 1964, was photographed at Bloxworth while operating route 91 in March 1969. *Phil Davies*

Above: **SANDBANKS** KEL 407 had entered service with Hants & Dorset in July 1950 as a Bristol L6G carrying a 28-seat coach body by Portsmouth Aviation. This body was later removed and the chassis lengthened to 30 feet in November 1961; a six-cylinder Bristol engine also replaced the previous Gardner unit, the vehicle thus becoming a Bristol LL6B. A new full-fronted Eastern Coach Works 39-seat bus body was fitted and KEL 407 re-entered service as a driver-only-operated bus in April 1962. This photograph was taken in April 1969, and the bus is seen disembarking from Sandbanks ferry while operating a through journey from Swanage to Bournemouth on route 7; notice the cutaway rear panelling so that the rear overhang of the bus will not ground on the ferry ramp at certain states of the tide. KEL 407 was withdrawn from service later in 1969. *Phil Davies*

Left: **BOURNEMOUTH BUS STATION** During the 1969 summer season it was still necessary to duplicate the single-deck through buses from Bournemouth to Swanage by running a double-deck between Bournemouth and Sandbanks so that through passengers could cross by ferry and join two waiting single-deck buses at Shell Bay. By 1969 many of the cream open-top buses had been withdrawn, and the vehicle provided for the Bournemouth to Sandbanks leg of the journey on this occasion was KEL 729, a Bristol KSW6B that had been new to Hants & Dorset in March 1951 and had been transferred from Southampton depot to Bournemouth depot in April 1969. Notice that the Swanage destination display now carries the additional information 'Change at Ferry'. *Neil Goodrich*

BOURNEMOUTH BUS STATION In 1956 Hants & Dorset had devised a system of colour-coded fleet number plates, which clearly indicated the depot at which each vehicle was allocated. Bristol LD6G RLJ 503, photographed at Bournemouth in the summer of 1969, has fleet number 1353 on a small rectangular orange plate, which shows that this bus was then allocated to Lymington depot. This system of colour-coded plates lasted until the fleet was renumbered in 1971, the colour codes being as follows:

Black figures on white background – Bournemouth
Black figures on blue background – Poole
Black figures on pink background – Ringwood
Black figures on orange background – Lymington
Black figures on yellow background – Southampton
Yellow figures on black background – Woolston
Black figures on green background – Fareham
Black figures on grey background – Eastleigh
White figures on blue background – Winchester

(When the system was first introduced there had also been white figures on a black background to denote Parkstone, but this had closed as an operational depot in September 1958, although the premises were retained by Hants & Dorset as an engineering base.)

RLJ 503 had been new to Hants & Dorset in July 1955 and remained in service with the company until December 1975. Here it is waiting at Bournemouth bus station to return to its home depot on route 121, which ran via Christchurch, Highcliffe, New Milton, Hordle and Wheel Inn. The red slip-board on the radiator reads 'Not on service for Bournemouth Corporation passengers' – this meant that on the outward journey from Bournemouth no passengers would be picked up between Bournemouth and Somerford (inclusive) unless they were travelling beyond Somerford Bridge, or were travelling to or from any bus stop in the Fairmile area between Cross Way and Grove Road East. This was part of an agreement between Hants & Dorset and Bournemouth Corporation Transport that dated back to 1935. *Neil Goodrich*

Below: **NEWGATE LANE, FAREHAM**
Part of the Hants & Dorset 73 route ran from Fareham to Lee-on-the-Solent via Peel Common and Stubbington; this low railway bridge, which carried the Gosport branch over Newgate Lane, illustrates why only single-deck buses could be used on this section of the route. Double-deck buses were often used on the other section of the 73 route between Fareham and Heathfield Estate, and any through passengers were required to change buses at Fareham. Bristol RELL6G PLJ 744G was photographed in October 1969; it had been new in May of that year. *Phil Davies*

Above: **BOURNEMOUTH BUS STATION** In June 1965 Hants & Dorset introduced limited-stop service 27 between Bournemouth and Southampton. This ran via Parley Cross, Ferndown, Ringwood, Cadnam and Totton, with an end-to-end running time of 85 minutes. Two Bristol FS double-deck buses were repainted in a cream livery with green wings to operate this route, which commenced in June 1965. In May 1969 the route was converted to driver-only single-deck operation, so the two double-deck buses previously used were transferred to other duties – retaining their cream livery at first. Bristol FS6G CEL 860C was caught by the camera at Bournemouth in the summer of 1969, operating route 18 to Barton-on-Sea via Christchurch, Mudeford and Highcliffe. This bus had entered traffic with Hants & Dorset in January 1965, so was only a few months old when repainted cream. It regained the normal green livery in June 1970, and was subsequently repainted in National Bus Company poppy red in November 1973. It remained in the Hants & Dorset fleet until March 1980. *Neil Goodrich*

THORNHILL ESTATE Hants & Dorset route 88/88A ran between Southampton Central railway station and Thornhill Estate via Bitterne. This was a very busy urban route and it is logical that it is seen here in November 1969 with a crew-operated 70-seat double-deck bus. Bristol FLF6B FLJ 153D had been new in February 1966, and remained in the Hants & Dorset fleet until the end of crew operation in November 1980. *Phil Davies*

ALDERHOLT MILL By complete contrast this photograph, taken in December 1969, illustrates one of Hants & Dorset's very rural routes. The 99 ran on Wednesdays only (Ringwood market day) from Cranborne to Ringwood via Cripplestyle, Crendell, Sandleheath and Alderholt. In 1969 the bus left Cranborne at 09.40, arriving in Ringwood at 10.41, while the return journey left Ringwood at 14.30 and terminated at Cranborne at 15.31. The afternoon return journey of this delightful bucolic operation is seen at Alderholt Mill, and this can be described as a Hants & Dorset photograph in every sense in that the photographer is standing in Hampshire while the bus is in Dorset. A converted Bristol MW6G saloon that was formerly a coach provides ample accommodation for this run. *Phil Davies*

GOSPORT It was in 1882 that the Provincial Tramways Company, which at that time also had operations in Cardiff, Devonport, Grimsby and Portsmouth, started a service of horse trams between Gosport Ferry and Ann's Hill. The Gosport tram network was extended and in due course electrified; electric tram services between Fareham railway station and Gosport commenced in January 1906. A tram depot and power generating plant had been built at Hoeford. The company began to operate motor buses in the Gosport area from 1910, and later also ran charabancs for tours and excursions. Tram operation in Fareham and Gosport ceased on 31 December 1929, all services thereafter being provided by motor buses, which operated from the former tram depot at Hoeford.

A significant event in the history of the company, which still traded as Provincial, was the appointment of Mr H. Orme White as Manager in 1936; he was in charge of the company for the following 30 years, and the operation came to very much reflect his personality. It was also in 1936 that the first double-deck buses entered the fleet; previously all motor buses had been saloons. Mr Orme White ensured that vehicles ran in service for many years, but at the same time he was an innovative person and between 1958 and 1967 a number of buses in the Provincial fleet were re-equipped with air-cooled engines. At the age of 81, Mr Orme White retired in December 1966, a Mr H. Woollford taking up the position of Managing Director from 1 January 1967. The parent company of Provincial was taken over by the Swain Group in 1969, which in turn sold the Gosport & Fareham operation to the

National Bus Company with effect from 1 January 1970. Management oversight was given to Hants & Dorset, although the Provincial name was retained. Steps were soon taken to bring a measure of standardisation to the rather unusual fleet, but for a year or two the Hants & Dorset-controlled Provincial fleet included some of the most remarkable buses to operate under the aegis of the National Bus Company.

This photograph epitomises the Provincial fleet as it was at the beginning of 1970. On the left 884 HHO is one of the Deutz engine rebuilds. The basis for this vehicle was a 1947 Guy Arab II chassis from a former Yorkshire Woollen District bus that had been acquired from a dealer in 1961. Following fitment of the Deutz engine the bus was given a new 56-seat highbridge body by Reading; it was re-registered 884 HHO and entered service in 1963, remaining in service until 1972. On the right, AEC Regal 4 saloon CG 9607 had been new to Provincial in 1934, originally carrying a Harrington body; it was given a new front-entrance body by Reading in 1962, thus making the vehicle suitable for driver-only operation. CG 9607 did not last very long into the era of Hants & Dorset control, being withdrawn during 1970. *The late Colin Caddy*

TOTTON The Hants & Dorset route 58 ran from Southampton to Langley and Lepe Beach via Redbridge, Totton, Eling, Marchwood and Hythe – most journeys continued from Langley to Lepe Beach during the summer, but terminated at Langley Tavern during the winter period. This photograph was taken in June 1970, and shows Bristol LD6G RLJ 508 on the A36 approaching Totton while operating from Southampton to Lepe Beach. New in September 1955, RLJ 508 was in service with Hants & Dorset until July 1975. *Phil Davies*

BOURNEMOUTH BUS STATION This photograph was also taken in June 1970, and Bristol RELL6G SRU 830H had only been in service for a few days. It was so new that it had not yet received its fleet number/depot allocation plate; a small temporarily applied fleet number can just be seen between the offside sidelight and the radiator. The brand-new vehicle is operating a route 6 journey from Bournemouth to Sandbanks, notwithstanding that Swanage is shown on the destination blind; notice the 'Change at Ferry' slipboard carried in the windscreen. *Phil Davies*

POOLE BUS STATION Work on building the Arndale (now Dolphin) shopping centre in Poole had started early in 1967, and Poole bus station was moved from Kingland Crescent to its current site in April of that year, initially with temporary stand arrangements and infrastructure. The Arndale Centre opened in 1970, and the bus station featured 14 'saw-tooth' bays. Photographed parked against the railings that separate the new bus station from Kingland Road we see LRU 52, a Bristol KSW6B with a 60-seat highbridge body, which had entered service with Hants & Dorset in June 1952. For many years highbridge Bristol KSWs operated the majority of Poole depot's town services – they were very popular with customers and crews alike. When this photograph was taken LRU 52 was nearing the end of its time with Hants & Dorset, being withdrawn from service in February 1971. The land on the other side of Kingland Road, just visible on the left of this photograph, was used a few years later to build Poole Arts Centre (now The Lighthouse). *Neil Goodrich*

POOLE BUS GARAGE Soon after the new Poole bus station opened, a bus parking area came into use between the shopping centre's multi-storey car park and the railway line, and a new maintenance depot was built into the lower rear section of the car park. Also provided was a new drive-through bus wash beside the entry road to the new garage. Highbridge-bodied Bristol KSW6B KRU 972 was photographed in the new bus wash in the spring of 1972; the appearance of the building housing it is little changed today. New to Hants & Dorset in December 1951, KRU 972 was in service with the company until September 1972. The opening of the new garage enabled the premises in Towngate Street/North Street, illustrated on page 8, to be closed, the site in due course being cleared for road improvements. *Neil Goodrich*

GROSVENOR SQUARE, SOUTHAMPTON

Like most large bus operators, Hants & Dorset operated its own driver training school. This provided suitably experienced direct entrants (e.g. lorry or van drivers) with the opportunity to gain what was then called a Public Service Vehicle (PSV) driving licence. Training was also offered to conductors over the age of 21 and with at least six months of service with the company, and in this way many conductors were able to become bus drivers.

Superannuated double-deck buses were used for driver training, and one of the most interesting to serve in this role was FRU 827. This Bristol K5G had joined the Hants & Dorset fleet in May 1946, and when delivered had carried the early post-war style of Eastern Coach Works lowbridge body. In March 1956 it was fitted with an older lowbridge body from a Hants & Dorset bus (APR 432) that had been new in May 1940. This had also been built by Eastern Coach Works, but was extensively rebuilt in Hants & Dorset's own workshops when transferred to FRU 827. Thus rebodied, the bus remained in the operational Hants & Dorset fleet until December 1963, then became a driver training vehicle in October 1964. After withdrawal from its training role, it was sold to a dealer in May 1972. This photograph at Grosvenor Square shows the withdrawn vehicle (note the 'Delicensed' sticker on the windscreen) just prior to being sold.
Neil Goodrich

HANTS & DORSET

BOURNEMOUTH BUS STATION Most journeys on the Hants & Dorset 16 route ran from New Milton via Highcliffe, Mudeford and Christchurch to Hurn Airport or Parley Cross; there were just a few journeys between Parley Cross and Bournemouth, which were in effect vehicle positioning movements, although they were available for any passengers who may have wished to travel on them. Bristol LS5G saloon SRU 976 had been operating on route 16 when photographed at Bournemouth bus station in the summer of 1972; new to Hants & Dorset in July 1956, this vehicle had been withdrawn in January 1972 but was reinstated in May of that year, continuing in service until final withdrawal in June 1974. *Neil Goodrich*

BOURNEMOUTH BUS STATION Lowbridge-bodied Bristol KSW6B KEL 728 had been new to Hants & Dorset in March 1951, and while in the company's operational fleet spent much of its time in the Southampton area, including a spell based at Lyndhurst outstation during the early 1950s. In December 1969 KEL 728 was converted to become a driver training bus. The open rear platform was panelled in and fitted with a sliding door as seen here, while the sunken upstairs gangway above the offside of the lower saloon was raised above the leading bay so that an instructor could stand behind the cab. Concrete blocks were located on each deck so that driving the bus felt as if it was carrying a number of passengers. After withdrawal from the training fleet, KEL 728 was sold in April 1976. *Neil Goodrich*

BOURNEMOUTH BUS STATION One of the more unusual designs of trucks was the Austin/Morris FG; the cab entry doors were set at an angle in the rear corners of the cab. This made getting in or out much easier for the driver if the truck was parked in a confined space, as the open door did not project beyond the width of the cab. SOW 272H had been purchased by Hants & Dorset in October 1969 and was used by the engineering department. Seen at Bournemouth bus station in the summer of 1972, it illustrates the yellow livery by then adopted for works vehicles; notice that both the Hants & Dorset (green background) and Wilts & Dorset (red background) fleet names are shown, acknowledging that the two fleets were now under common management. *Neil Goodrich*

POOLE BUS STATION When Hants & Dorset had been given management oversight of the Gosport & Fareham Omnibus Company (Provincial) at the beginning of 1970, Provincial had on order six Daimler Fleetline double-deck buses with 74-seat bodywork by Roe, suitable for driver-only operation. The six were not delivered until well into 1971, and by this time it had been decided that they would become part of the Hants & Dorset fleet in exchange for six newly delivered Bristol RE single-deck buses. Four of the six Daimlers were allocated to Poole depot, the other two going initially to Southampton but later also being transferred to Poole. These were the first driver-only-operated double-deck buses for Hants & Dorset, and the initial allocation to Poole enabled all journeys on route 1 (Poole-Bournemouth via Lower Parkstone and Penn Hill) to be converted to driver-only operation, together with evening and Sunday journeys on route 2 (Poole-Bournemouth via Lower Parkstone and Bournemouth Road). The first of the batch, VRU 124J, is seen when newly in service at Poole bus station in July 1971, parked against the railings and ready to operate a journey on route 1 between Poole and Bournemouth. *Phil Davies*

HANTS & DORSET

Right: **BOURNEMOUTH BUS STATION** Weekday daytime journeys on route 2 between Poole and Bournemouth remained crew-operated until 1974. This photograph, taken at Bournemouth bus station in 1972, shows Bristol KSW6G LRU 57 awaiting departure time to return to Poole on route 2 – the rear of a Daimler on route 1 can just be seen on the stand in front. New to Hants & Dorset in November 1952, LRU 57 was in due course to be the very last of the popular Bristol KSW highbridge buses to remain in service at Poole depot, finally being withdrawn in September 1974; the last Bristol KSW highbridge of all in the Hants & Dorset fleet was LRU 61, which was withdrawn from Fareham depot in November 1974. *Neil Goodrich*

Left: **BOURNEMOUTH BUS STATION** The Hants & Dorset and Wilts & Dorset fleets were renumbered from September 1971, with the new numbers being allocated in blocks by vehicle type. The system of showing depot allocations by means of coloured fleet number plates, as described on page 11, was abolished in favour of coloured adhesive discs to convey this information. When this photograph was taken in 1972 Bristol LD6G RLJ 504 (left) had recently been transferred from Southampton to Bournemouth depot, but still carries a single yellow disc indicating a Southampton allocation. This may have been intentional, because the bus in question was very soon transferred on to Poole depot, where it remained until transferred back to Southampton during 1974. Having been new in July 1955, RLJ 504 was in service with the company until May 1976. Bristol MW6G 2689 RU on the right had been new as a coach in April 1963; it was fitted with the bus-style destination blind in December 1971 but retained coach livery until 1973 when it was painted NBC poppy red and fitted with bus seats. It was withdrawn in December 1975. When photographed here it was being used on the works contract service to Winfrith AEE. *Neil Goodrich*

BOURNEMOUTH BUS STATION Carrying trade plates 074 OW when photographed in 1972, this AEC Matador had been acquired by Wilts & Dorset Motor Services from the Ministry of Supply in January 1960; Wilts & Dorset then rebuilt it as a recovery vehicle in its own workshops in November 1960. It was transferred to the Hants & Dorset fleet in January 1972, and is seen in use later that year.

As from 1 January 1969 the National Bus Company had come into being, bringing into one organisation all of the Transport Holding Company bus operations together with what had been the BET companies in the UK. At first there were few visible effects for Hants & Dorset, but from 1972 onwards many changes were to occur.
Neil Goodrich

POOLE BUS GARAGE Management of Hants & Dorset Motor Services and Wilts & Dorset Motor Services had been progressively merged from 1964 onwards. It was decided that from October 1972 the entire operation would trade as Hants & Dorset. This meant that the Hants & Dorset name would soon be seen on the sides of buses operated from the former Wilts & Dorset depots at Salisbury, Pewsey, Andover and Basingstoke as well as at a number of outstations in various parts of rural Wiltshire. Wilts & Dorset buses had been red for many years, while those operated by Hants & Dorset had traditionally been green. The decision was taken that the livery for the enlarged Hants & Dorset operation would be National Bus Company poppy red; thus bus users in the former Wilts & Dorset area still had red buses (albeit a different shade), but had to get used to a new name, while people in the Hants & Dorset area retained the familiar name but the buses were, over the next few years, repainted red.

Hants & Dorset's first Bristol VRT double-deck buses with 74-seat Eastern Coach Works bodies were delivered towards the end of 1972, with the intention that they would enter traffic at Basingstoke from 1 January 1973. In the event one of the batch, CRU 304L, was pressed into service at Poole for a couple of weeks during December 1972. These photographs were taken at Poole bus garage, and show CRU 304L in poppy red livery and sporting Basingstoke depot blue and black allocation discs. Notice the temporary Poole-Bournemouth destination display that had been fitted; as the bus was intended only to be used on route 1 while at Poole it was not considered necessary to fit a Poole depot destination blind.

The rear view of CRU 304L is also of interest, showing the neat styling of the body of the Series 2 VRT, which did not have to accommodate the high-level ventilation grills fitted to the Series 3 VRTs. The bus is powered by a Gardner 6LX engine mounted transversely at the rear. *Both the late H. Stevens, courtesy of Julia Stevens*

BASINGSTOKE As well as the livery change, the National Bus Company also decreed that corporate-identity-style fleet names should be applied to buses and coaches; this was to be done irrespective of whether or not the vehicle had been repainted in the new livery. It is likely that HMW 447, a Bristol KSW5G that had been new to Wilts & Dorset in 1952, was one of the first buses at Basingstoke to get the new name as, together with the National Bus Company logo, it has been fitted near the centre of the lower deck body, in the same position that would have been occupied by the old Tilling-style fleet name – the correct position for the new logo and name was further forward, as demonstrated by the Bristol FS double deck parked behind HMW 447 in this photograph, which was taken early in 1973. The advertisement between the decks proclaims 'Part of the National Bus Company. Together we're really going places'. HMW 447 did not go very much further, being withdrawn later that year. *The late H. Stevens, courtesy of Julia Stevens*

BASINGSTOKE It may seem slightly odd that an undertaking called Wilts & Dorset had been operating buses in and around Basingstoke on routes that went nowhere near either of the two counties in the company's title. From 1926 until 1950 bus services in Basingstoke were operated by Venture, which by the late 1940s was part of Red & White United Transport. Red & White sold out to the British Transport Commission in 1950, and the BTC placed Venture under the control of Wilts & Dorset from 1 January 1951. The Venture name soon disappeared, but it would in due course be seen again between 1979 and 1983 – see page 45. The bus station and garage at Basingstoke seen in this photograph had been provided by Wilts & Dorset and opened in June 1962. This photograph was taken in the spring of 1973 and it can be seen that the Hants & Dorset fleet name has been applied to most of the vehicles, although the Bristol RELL saloon centre right still sports a Tilling-style Wilts & Dorset fleet name. *The late H. Stevens, courtesy of Julia Stevens*

POOLE BUS STATION Eastern Coach Works developed and improved the body design of the Bristol LH single-deck bus; the appearance of the class was particularly enhanced by the adoption of the BET-style curved windscreen, which started to be seen in production models from mid-1971 onwards. Bristol LH6L NLJ 516M, seen here driving through the bus station, entered traffic with Hants & Dorset in 1973, and is seen during November of that year – compare the front of this bus with that of NLJ 817G illustrated on page 9. When new, NLJ 516M was allocated to Bere Regis outstation, where it was used on route 11A (Bere Regis-Dorchester) and routes 90/91 (Poole-Bere Regis). In these photographs it is operating the 12.45 route 90 journey from Poole to Winterborne Kingston, and is carrying a good load of passengers; in the early/mid-1970s the 16.35 journey

from Poole to Winterborne Kingston on route 90 was still crew-operated by Poole depot, and the numbers using it regularly filled a 60-seat double-deck bus. NLJ 516M was later transferred to Bournemouth depot, then to Blandford, where its body was subsequently severely damaged in a road traffic accident at Blandford Camp during adverse weather conditions. However, this was not the end of the road for this vehicle, as we will see on page 46.

On the left Bristol FLF6G GRU 976D can be seen parked against the railings, marked up ready to operate a journey on route 28, which ran from Poole to Westbourne via Oakdale, Newtown, Alderney, Wallisdown, Alder Road and Branksome. New to Hants & Dorset in August 1966, GRU 976D was in service with the company until September 1980. *Both Phil Davies*

POOLE BUS GARAGE Long delays in the deliveries of previously ordered new buses meant that Hants & Dorset was seriously short of vehicles by 1974. One of the ways in which this was remedied was by hiring in buses from other operators, including the local municipal operator Bournemouth Corporation Transport. Leyland PD3 8153 EL was one of six double-deck buses of this type that were used by Hants & Dorset for various periods between June 1974 and January 1975. This bus had been new to Bournemouth Corporation Transport in 1960 and carried a 62-seat body by Weymann, which featured a rear entrance/front exit layout, with two staircases; it was photographed at Poole bus garage in September 1974. Obviously care had to be taken to avoid these yellow-liveried buses running on routes into Bournemouth; in practice they were used mostly on schools and works services, which had the valuable function of freeing up Hants & Dorset-liveried vehicles for service work. Among other vehicles hired in at this time were some Devon General AEC Regent V double-deck buses, which were seen for a few weeks on a number of routes operated from Poole depot. *Brian Jackson*

POOLE BUS STATION Hants & Dorset also found it necessary to purchase a number of second-hand buses during the early 1970s. 532 HKJ was one of a batch of six Leyland Atlanteans bought from Maidstone & District in March 1973; in the event only five of them were used in service by Hants & Dorset, and by the time they had been repainted into National Bus Company poppy red livery the first examples did not enter traffic with the company until 1974. 532 HKJ had been new to Maidstone & District in 1960 and while in service with Hants & Dorset carried 75 seats in its MCCW body (reduced from the 77 seats it had while in service with Maidstone & District); it is seen resting between trips at Poole bus station in 1974. By mid-1975 532 HKJ had been transferred to Basingstoke depot, and it was subsequently withdrawn from service in December 1976. *The late D. Habgood*

HANTS & DORSET

Right: **UPAVON** was for many years a connection point for Wilts & Dorset bus services running between Salisbury and Marlborough or Devizes. This photograph was taken in late 1974 and shows the crew of a Bristol FS on route 210 from Devizes standing in the time-honoured way in front of their vehicle, while passengers board a Bristol MW on route 205 to Marlborough. The vehicles now carry Hants & Dorset fleet names in the approved National Bus Company corporate style, but it can be seen that a Tilling-style Wilts & Dorset fleet name remains in place above the radiator grille of the Bristol MW. *Brian Jackson*

Below: **SALISBURY BUS STATION** Three interesting vehicles were caught by the camera parked at the Rollestone Street end of Salisbury bus station on a wet day in May 1975. On the left of the line-up is LMR 733F, a Bedford VAL70 coach new to Wilts & Dorset in 1968 and carrying a 49-seat Duple (Northern) body. In the centre is Bristol MW6G/Eastern Coach Works 41-seat dual-purpose saloon 134 AMW, which had been new in 1963. It is marked up for route 256, which was an infrequent local service between Salisbury and Netherhampton. On the right RRU 582N is a Ford R1014 carrying a 45-seat Eastern Coach Works single-deck bus body. The design of the body is very similar to those produced for the Bristol LH, but with an extra bay at the rear. Looking at the destination blind, RRU 582N – which had entered traffic in 1974 – had recently operated a journey into Salisbury on route 244 from Woodfalls and Morgan's Vale. Salisbury bus station had been opened by Wilts & Dorset in 1939 and remained in use until January 2014. *Brian Jackson*

PEWSEY The Salisbury-based Wilts & Dorset Motor Services had taken over the services of Lampard's Garages of Pewsey in November 1944. No vehicles were acquired, but six routes in the local area were transferred to Wilts & Dorset, which established a depot at Frog Meadow. This depot is seen in the summer of 1975, after Wilts & Dorset had been subsumed into Hants & Dorset – notice the Hants & Dorset name in white letters on a blue background above the two poster cases in the left foreground. Parked in the depot we see three Eastern Coach Works-bodied Ford R1014s together with a Bristol LH6L that had been new to Wilts & Dorset in 1970; TRU 227J (third from left) is easily distinguishable by its flat windscreen. In the 21st century these premises at Frog Meadow are no longer in use as a bus depot. *Brian Jackson*

Below: **ASHLEY ROAD, UPPER PARKSTONE** On the right of this photograph, taken on an autumn day in 1975, we see Bristol LD6G UEL 710 picking up passengers for Bournemouth at the St John's Church bus stop in Ashley Road, Upper Parkstone. UEL 710 was in service with Hants & Dorset from November 1957 until May 1976. On the opposite side of the road is Hants & Dorset's Parkstone booking office; this building dated back to the days of the former municipal tram depot at the rear of the site, although the shop front had been modernised during the 1950s. The roadway by the side of the booking office led to the depot, which had been acquired by Hants & Dorset after the demise of the trams in 1935; it ceased to be used as an operational bus depot in September 1958, with buses and crews moving to Poole and Bournemouth depots, but an engineering workshop was retained here until the late 1970s. The booking office survived rather longer, and a replacement was provided when the site was developed as part of the Safeway (now Waitrose) supermarket in the 1980s. The replacement booking office closed in 2006, and at the time of writing is used as a barber's shop. *Hants & Dorset*

Above: **EASTLEIGH BUS STATION** By the time this photograph was taken at Eastleigh bus station, Blenheim Road, it could be seen that considerable progress had been made in repainting the Hants & Dorset fleet into National Bus Company poppy red livery. A total of 33 second-hand Leyland Panther saloons had joined the fleet late in 1971, entering service during 1972. Two of those acquired are included in this photograph. Closest to the camera is DKE 265C, which had been new to Maidstone & District in 1965 and which continued in service with Hants & Dorset until May 1977. On the extreme right of the photograph is Bristol FLF6G GLJ 750D, which was new to Hants & Dorset in June 1966 and remained in the fleet until November 1980. Eastleigh bus station was subsequently moved from Blenheim Road to its present location at Upper Market Street in July 1976; Portakabin offices were used for the first few years at the Upper Market Street location. *Brian Jackson*

WAREHAM STATION With effect from 1 January 1974 the Western National garage and operations at Swanage had been passed to Hants & Dorset. The only former Western National vehicle that Hants & Dorset retained for more than a few months was LDV 459F, a Bristol RELL6G that had entered traffic with its former owner in 1968. Here it is seen in the early summer of 1976 at Wareham station, providing the connection on route 142 via Corfe Castle and Harmans Cross onwards to Swanage; at the time of writing all Poole-Wareham-Swanage journeys on 'Purbeck Breezer' route 40 run via Corfe Castle, Kingston and Langton Matravers. LDV 459F was in service with Hants & Dorset until March 1983. *Brian Jackson*

BOURNEMOUTH BUS STATION During the early hours of Sunday 25 July 1976 Bournemouth bus station was devastated by a fire so fierce that the crew of a ship some way out at sea radioed ashore to query the 'strange light' that could be seen over Bournemouth. It was indeed fortunate that the buses parked for the night on the upper level were quickly driven to safety in nearby streets, in many cases by members of the public who happened to be in Bournemouth town centre – some staff later had to walk around the town to find some of them. This photograph, looking down Exeter Crescent from Exeter Road, was taken a few days after the blaze. The smoke-blackened entrance in the centre of the photograph took pedestrians into the coach station, with stairs immediately on the left leading to the bus station on the upper level. *Brian Jackson*

Left: **BOURNEMOUTH BUS STATION** Photographed looking across Exeter Crescent from Eden Glen, this picture shows the vehicle exit from the ground-level coach station; note the severe cracking to the wall on the left, illustrating the tremendous heat that had been generated by the fire. This ensured that only a small portion of the bus station, which was on solid ground near Exeter Road, was ever used again, together with the largely undamaged office block. It was to everybody's great credit that a full bus service ran on the Sunday morning and on succeeding days; the effect of the conflagration on Hants & Dorset's coach tours and excursions programme was more significant as eight of Bournemouth depot's allocation of 11 coaches had been destroyed in the fire. Nonetheless by the middle of the following week various coaches had been brought in from other depots, enabling the advertised programme to run again. *Brian Jackson*

Right: **BOURNEMOUTH** In the aftermath of the July 1976 fire one of the most pressing problems was the establishment of an alternative terminus point for Hants & Dorset buses in Bournemouth. As an emergency measure the forecourt of Bournemouth Town Hall in Bourne Avenue was used on Sunday 25 July, but from the following day a temporary terminus was established at Bournemouth Triangle, which in fact remained in this role for a number of years, becoming a significant travel interchange point. The green open-top bus, RPN 9, seen here waiting time to depart from the Triangle for Sandbanks on route 148, is a Bristol FS6B that had been new to Brighton, Hove & District in 1959 and which had been purchased, together with three very similar LDS6Bs, by Hants & Dorset from Southdown in 1976, bringing a welcome return of open-top buses to the Sandbanks routes for a couple of summer seasons. RPN 9 was withdrawn by Hants & Dorset at the end of August 1977. *Brian Jackson*

MALLARD ROAD, BOURNEMOUTH The other immediate issue was overnight parking arrangements for the Bournemouth depot vehicles. Fortunately Bournemouth Transport allowed Hants & Dorset to use some of the space at its Mallard Road premises for vehicle parking as a temporary expedient (the arrangement lasted for a couple of years). Closest to the camera in this photograph, taken at Mallard Road in July 1976, is Bristol LH6L ORU 530M, which had been new in May 1974 and had the lower front bodywork modified for operation to and from Swanage via Sandbanks Ferry, but in this instance is marked up ready to operate a works contract journey to Winfrith. Partly visible in the right background is one of the Bristol LDS6B open-tops purchased by Hants & Dorset from Southdown in 1976. *Brian Jackson*

BOURNEMOUTH BUS STATION By early 1977 the area of Bournemouth bus station that was built on solid ground beside Exeter Road had been brought back into use, with departure stands provided for a number of westbound services from the town. This photograph was taken on 22 January 1977 and shows Bristol VRT NRU 311M ready to depart for Poole via Penn Hill on route 1. This was one of two Hants & Dorset Bristol VRTs that were given a special livery to celebrate the Silver Jubilee of Her Majesty the Queen. In this instance, the special livery had been sponsored by Beales/Bealesons. Beales was a major department store in Bournemouth that finally closed in March 2020. *David Pennels*

WEYMOUTH BUS GARAGE The other Hants & Dorset Bristol VRT that was given a Silver Jubilee livery in 1977 was NRU 307M. For this vehicle the livery was sponsored by Kennedy's, a builders' merchants based in Holdenhurst Road, Bournemouth, with branches in a number of locations including Poole, Southampton, Andover and New Milton. Kennedy's was bought out by Travis Perkins in the late 1980s; subsequently the former main building in Holdenhurst Road, Bournemouth, was demolished and the site is now in retail use. When photographed here NRU 307M had been temporarily loaned to Western National at Weymouth to take part in a special event. *Brian Jackson*

SWANAGE In 1973 Hants & Dorset had taken over the routes and vehicles of King Alfred Motor Services, which had operated in the Winchester area. Among the 37 vehicles taken over were four Leyland Atlantean double-deck buses, which were in due course transferred to Swanage and Poole depots, largely for school contract work. HOR 591E (left) and HOR 590E are seen parked between duties at Swanage in 1977. New to King Alfred in April 1967, these buses had passed to Hants & Dorset in April 1973 and would subsequently transfer to the Bristol Omnibus Company in 1979. *Brian Jackson*

BOURNE AVENUE, BOURNEMOUTH Sunday 26 February 1978 saw the largest reorganisation of the bus network in the Poole and Bournemouth area since 1954, with greatly altered routes and new route numbers. One of the new routes introduced at that time was the 160, which ran from Bournemouth to Poole via Surrey Road, Bourne Valley, Bourne Estate, Alderney and Oakdale. On 26 July 1978 Bristol FLF6B DEL 893C was caught by the camera in Bourne Avenue shortly after commencing the journey from Bournemouth to Poole. New in June 1965, DEL 893C was in service with Hants & Dorset until August 1980. The gateway that the bus is passing is a pedestrian access to Richmond Hill St Andrew's United Reformed Church, a beautiful building dating from 1891 and, with seating for more than 1,000, thought to have the largest capacity of any church in Bournemouth; it was known for many years as the 'Cathedral of Congregationalism'. *Neil Goodrich*

EDEN GLEN, BOURNEMOUTH Hants & Dorset had been acquiring second-hand coaches well before the Bournemouth fire, with vehicles coming into the fleet from Southdown and North Western. Alexander-bodied Leyland Leopard AJA 149B had been new to North Western in 1964 and was acquired by Hants & Dorset in May 1975. When photographed at Eden Glen, Bournemouth, on 30 July 1978 it was carrying blue and orange depot allocation discs, indicating that it was then based at Andover. By this time its days in the Hants & Dorset fleet were numbered – it was withdrawn in September 1978. *Neil Goodrich*

RUTLAND ROAD, BOURNEMOUTH Following the disastrous fire at Bournemouth, Hants & Dorset re-purchased the old Norwich Avenue premises that had previously served as Bournemouth depot until 1959, and also later made use of the former Royal Blue depot in Rutland Road, Bournemouth. Seen receiving attention at Rutland Road on 3 August 1978 is NJT 830P, one of the batch of five Plaxton-bodied Ford saloons that joined the Hants & Dorset fleet in 1976; even with the front panelling removed, the bodywork can be seen to differ from the examples bodied by Eastern Coach Works. Hants & Dorset subsequently purchased the Rutland Road premises from Western National in March 1980, but the company's ownership did not continue for long; the sheds at Rutland Road could only be used to service single-deck vehicles, and were also located in a residential area. Hants & Dorset vacated Rutland Road in December 1980 and the site was sold in November the following year. *Neil Goodrich*

EDEN GLEN, BOURNEMOUTH Carrying the yellow livery prescribed during the National Bus Company era, these three Hants & Dorset driver training buses at Eden Glen on 9 August 1978 are all slightly different. On the left, YRU 65 is a Bristol LD6G that had been new to Hants & Dorset in October 1959 and was converted for use as a training bus in April 1976. In the centre, 5678 EL is a Bristol FS6G that had entered service with Hants & Dorset in February 1961, becoming a driver training bus in March 1978. Finally, on the right is XPM 48, a Bristol FS6B that had started life with Brighton, Hove & District in 1962 and had come to Hants & Dorset in June 1974. This bus was withdrawn from the passenger-carrying fleet in March 1978 and converted for use in driver training (normally based at Hoeford) in June 1978. The driving tuition provided by Hants & Dorset was of the highest standard; with a steady movement toward driver-only operation in the late 1970s there was an emphasis on teaching existing conductors to drive, and a number of conductors were trained from being provisional licence holders to full PSV standard at this time. *Neil Goodrich*

ST MICHAEL'S ROUNDABOUT, BOURNEMOUTH
Further second-hand acquisitions in 1974 had brought a different type of the Bristol/Eastern Coach Works Lodekka into the Hants & Dorset fleet. Four Bristol FSF6Bs that had been new to Brighton, Hove & District in 1962 were acquired via Southdown and were repainted in poppy red livery before entering service with Hants & Dorset during 1975. Illustrating this unusual type in the Hants & Dorset fleet, WNJ 40 was photographed approaching St Michael's Roundabout in Bournemouth while operating a journey to Poole on route 103 on 9 August 1978. The 103 route had been introduced with the reorganisation of the Poole area bus network in February 1978 and ran from Bournemouth to Poole via Westbourne, Branksome, Upper Parkstone and Lower Parkstone. When this photograph was taken WNJ 40 was nearing the end its short time in the Hants & Dorset fleet, being withdrawn from service in October 1978. *Neil Goodrich*

EDEN GLEN, BOURNEMOUTH This photograph, taken on 27 August 1978, nicely illustrates how the Eastern Coach Works body for the Bristol LH single-deck bus was developed. On the right we see ULJ 368J, which had been new to Hants & Dorset in 1970. The general body design of this vehicle is quite similar to that of Hants & Dorset's first Bristol LH, which is illustrated on page 9, although it will be noted that the windscreen fitted to ULJ 368J is deeper than that of the earlier vehicle; the original design had been particularly shallow and was not satisfactory, especially for taller drivers.

On the left is ORU 531M, which was new in May 1974. Immediately noticeable is the curved BET-style windscreen, which many people felt made for a more attractive and modern-looking vehicle. The cut-away front panelling is to allow clearance on and off the Sandbanks ferry when operating between Bournemouth and Swanage, although when this photograph was taken ORU 531M had recently operated a route 139 journey between Shaftesbury and Bournemouth. *Neil Goodrich*

WEYMOUTH The Leyland National single-deck bus was developed as a joint project by Leyland Motors and the National Bus Company. Large quantities were produced between 1972 and 1985 at a factory in Workington that had been built especially for this purpose, and the Leyland National was seen widely across the various National Bus Company operating fleets. Hants & Dorset received its first Leyland Nationals in 1973; NEL 856M had been new in December of that year. It was caught by the camera in Weymouth on 30 August 1978, marked up ready to operate a route 437 journey back to Bournemouth via Dorchester, Affpuddle, Bere Regis and Poole. Notice the green Western National Bristol FLF double-deck buses partly visible parked up in the right background. *Neil Goodrich*

WEYMOUTH Routes 434 and 435 ran between Salisbury and Weymouth via Blandford, the service between Salisbury and Weymouth having been established by Wilts & Dorset in 1929. Appropriately the bus that we see here in the Western National bus garage at Weymouth on 30 August 1978, Bristol RELL6G RLJ 797H, had been new to Salisbury-based Wilts & Dorset in October 1969, and had taken the Hants & Dorset name after Wilts & Dorset had been subsumed into that company in October 1972. The 435 route ran via Blandford Camp, with a journey time of around 2 hours 15 minutes between Salisbury and Weymouth. *Neil Goodrich*

EDEN GLEN, BOURNEMOUTH New to Hants & Dorset in April 1974, ORU 382M was a Leyland PSU3B/4R coach carrying a Plaxton body seating 44 passengers. Although allocated to Bournemouth at the time of the disastrous 1976 fire, it was fortuitously away from the depot on that dreadful July night and thus avoided destruction. Photographed at Eden Glen, Bournemouth, on 17 September 1978, the coach is in the prescribed National white livery and carrying Hants & Dorset fleet names. When Hants & Dorset was subsequently broken up in 1983, ORU 382M was allocated to the Shamrock & Rambler fleet. Later a new company, Pilgrim Coaches, was formed in January 1984 by the National Bus Company, and took over the Southampton operations of Shamrock & Rambler. ORU 382M became part of the Pilgrim fleet from January 1984 until withdrawal in February 1986. The Pilgrim Coaches operation only lasted a little longer; its operations, which had been based at Grosvenor Square, Southampton, ceased in April 1987. *Neil Goodrich*

Right: **ST MICHAEL'S ROUNDABOUT, BOURNEMOUTH**
Another of the new routes that had been introduced as part of the revised bus network in the Poole and Bournemouth area from February 1978 was the 106, which ran from Bournemouth to Creekmoor via Upper Parkstone, Sea View, Foxholes Estate and Oakdale. Photographed approaching St Michael's Roundabout on 24 November 1978 is Bristol VRT MEL 559P. This bus had been new to Hants & Dorset in January 1976; it had been given the rather startling overall livery illustrated here in the spring of 1978 to promote Poole Arts Centre. Built in Kingland Road opposite Poole bus station, the Arts Centre has been described by Arts Council England as the largest in the UK outside London, and was opened in April 1978. Following a major refurbishment in 2002, the building was renamed Lighthouse, Poole's Centre for the Arts, and remains a very popular attraction. *Neil Goodrich*

Left: **ST MICHAEL'S ROUNDABOUT, BOURNEMOUTH**
This photograph was taken from a slightly different angle compared with the previous one, and therefore includes part of the church that gives the roundabout its name. St Michael's Church is a landmark when approaching Bournemouth from the west; the main building, dating from 1873-76, was designed by Norman Shaw, while the large tower was added in 1900-01, to the design of John Oldrid Scott.

Bristol FS6B 474 BMR had been new to Salisbury-based Wilts & Dorset Motor Services in January 1964, becoming part of the enlarged Hants & Dorset fleet in 1972. Because in general greater progress had been made towards converting to driver-only operation in the erstwhile Wilts & Dorset area, a number of relatively modern crew-operated buses were transferred south to see out their final days with the company and to replace older Hants & Dorset stock. When caught by the camera on 24 November 1978 474 BMR was operating on route 169 from Bournemouth to Wallisdown via Branksome, Bourne Valley, Bourne Estate and Alder Road. The bus remained in service with Hants & Dorset until June 1980. *Neil Goodrich*

Left: **RINGWOOD BUS DEPOT** The winter of 1978-79 will be remembered as the 'Winter of Discontent' owing to a series of strikes by such employees as refuse collectors, lorry drivers and school caretakers, which by early 1979 added up to the largest labour stoppage in Britain since the General Strike of 1926. The situation was exacerbated by a period of exceptionally cold weather, with snowfalls occurring in many parts of the country. It can be seen that there was snow on the ground when this photograph was taken at Ringwood bus depot on 31 December 1978; Leyland National GLJ 676N, seen as the day is just getting light, awaits its next call to duty. This vehicle had entered traffic with Hants & Dorset in January 1975 and was dual-purpose with 48 semi-coach seats. The company endeavoured to use this type of vehicle on the longer limited-stop routes – as demonstrated by GLJ 676N, which has recently operated on route X27, which ran between Bournemouth and Southampton via Ringwood and Cadnam. *Neil Goodrich*

Right: **POOLE BUS GARAGE** This photograph of Bristol LDS6B OPN 801 was taken at Poole on 1 January 1979 after this former Brighton, Hove & District convertible open-top, acquired by Hants & Dorset in 1976, had been adapted in November 1978 for use as a tree-cutting bus. Overhanging trees obstructing the highway can cause serious damage to double-deck buses, and for many years Hants & Dorset allocated a vehicle to tree-cutting work to ensure the safety of customers, staff and vehicles. The staff who looked after bus stops and roadside timetable displays were generally those who also undertook tree-cutting. Nonetheless, it is suspected that few, if any, trees were cut on the bitterly cold morning of 1 January 1979. *Neil Goodrich*

LYNDHURST When Hants & Dorset had acquired King Alfred Motor Services of Winchester in April 1973 (see also page 34), among the vehicles to join the company's fleet was BCG 701J, a Bedford YRQ coach carrying a 45-seat body by Duple. This coach had entered service with King Alfred in June 1971, and by the time this photograph was taken at Lyndhurst on 22 January 1979 it had been painted into the overall white livery prescribed by the National Bus Company for coaches operated by the subsidiary companies. *Neil Goodrich*

TOTTON Although by 1979 regular deliveries of new buses meant that Hants & Dorset was far better placed for vehicles than had been the case in the middle of that decade, a hiatus in the delivery of new Bristol VRT double-deck buses between October 1978 and February 1979 made it necessary to hire seven Leyland Atlantean double-deck buses from Portsmouth City Transport from December 1978 until March 1979. These hired-in vehicles are exemplified by 224 BTP, which had been new to Portsmouth in 1963 and was caught by the camera in Totton while with Hants & Dorset on Monday 22 January 1979; as nothing is shown on the destination blind, it is likely that the vehicle is operating a school contract journey. *Neil Goodrich*

HOEFORD New to Hants & Dorset in May 1976, Bristol VRT NEL 117P had 70 comfortable semi-coach seats in its Eastern Coach Works body and as such was painted in the dual-purpose poppy red and white livery. When photographed on January 1979 it was undergoing a chassis clean at Hoeford, which was originally the Provincial depot (see also page 15 for the explanation of how these premises passed to Hants & Dorset). Its number blind shows route X71, which was the 'Solenteer' service; operated jointly by Hants & Dorset and Southdown, this had been introduced in 1976 and linked Southampton with Portsmouth and Southsea. The yellow and black discs above the fleet number show that NEL 117P was allocated to Hants & Dorset's Fareham depot. *Neil Goodrich*

COMMERCIAL ROAD, BOURNEMOUTH Late in 1977 Hants & Dorset had received a batch of six Bristol VRTs with detachable roofs, although the only time that these buses were used in open-top format while in Hants & Dorset ownership was for the 1978 Derby. When delivered they were painted in poppy red livery and at a quick glance looked like standard buses, although the sharp-eyed could discern that they were convertible by observing the detachment line around the body below the upper deck windows and the lifting lugs on the edge of the roof. UFX 855S is seen picking up passengers for Poole in Commercial Road, Bournemouth, when newly in service with Hants & Dorset; this photograph has deliberately been placed slightly out of chronological order so that we can illustrate the full story of this batch of vehicles together. *Hants & Dorset*

HANTS & DORSET

Left: **EAST COWES** During the spring of 1979 Hants & Dorset's six convertible Bristol VRTs were exchanged for six conventional Bristol VRTs from the Southern Vectis fleet. On 21 April 1979 UFX 856S disembarks from the Red Funnel ferry *Netley Castle* at East Cowes as ferry staff (and the bus driver) carefully check ground clearances. Built by Ryton Marine at Wallsend, Tyne, MV *Netley Castle* had entered service with Red Funnel in 1974 and was in that company's fleet until 1996; sold after withdrawal from service, at the time of writing (2020) the vessel is believed to be still in service in Croatia. *Neil Goodrich*

Left: **NEWPORT, ISLE OF WIGHT** The exchanged Hants & Dorset buses were quickly placed in service by Southern Vectis after arrival on the Isle of Wight. This photograph was also taken on 21 April 1979 and shows UFX 855S operating on Southern Vectis route 1B from Newport to Cowes. Compare this photograph of the vehicle in green and white livery with that of the same bus in poppy red on the opposite page. *Neil Goodrich*

SOUTHAMPTON The six standard Southern Vectis Bristol VRTs that were exchanged for Hants & Dorset's convertible open-top buses were registered UDL 671S to UDL 676S inclusive, and had entered service with Southern Vectis in May 1978. As the Hants & Dorset buses were taken to the island, similarly the Southern Vectis vehicles came to the mainland to take up their new duties with Hants & Dorset; UDL 674S is seen disembarking from MV *Netley Castle* on 23 April 1979. *Neil Goodrich*

ST MICHAEL'S ROUNDABOUT, BOURNEMOUTH The convertible open-top buses sent by Hants & Dorset to the Isle of Wight were a few months older than the conventional Southern Vectis Bristol VRTs received in exchange. It was therefore agreed that Hants & Dorset would, as we have seen in the photographs, repaint the outgoing buses green prior to the exchange, but would receive the incoming buses in National Bus Company leaf green livery. As things turned out the buses received from the Isle of Wight ran for some time in this livery in the Poole and Bournemouth area, perhaps offering a glimpse of what might have been had Hants & Dorset retained green livery in 1972 instead of opting for NBC poppy red. UDL 671S is seen approaching St Michael's Roundabout, nearing journey's end while operating a route 103 journey from Poole on 28 April 1979. *Neil Goodrich*

WINCHESTER ROAD, SOUTHAMPTON Garage premises in Winchester Road, Southampton, served Hants & Dorset as a body shop until May 1979, when this activity was transferred to the company's new central repair works at Barton Park, Eastleigh, which was officially opened in May 1981. Here is a glimpse inside the Winchester Road body shop on 23 April 1979, shortly before the move to Barton Park. Closest to the camera, Leyland PSU3/4R coach CRN 832D receives attention; a dual-purpose Leyland National can be seen in the background. Carrying a 49-seat coach body by Plaxton, CRN 832D had been new to Ribble in 1966 and had passed to Hants & Dorset in March 1977. Notwithstanding the repair work being carried out here, this vehicle was nearing the end of its time in the Hants & Dorset fleet, being withdrawn in June 1979. Hants & Dorset had acquired the Winchester Road premises in 1935 with the purchase of the excursions & tours section of B. H. Ransome's Southampton-based Tourist Motor Coaches Limited. *Neil Goodrich*

GROSVENOR SQUARE, SOUTHAMPTON This view of the interior of the lower deck of Bristol FS6G BEL 679B, taken on 23 April 1979, nicely captures the atmosphere of travelling on crew-operated Hants & Dorset buses in the late 1970s. BEL 679B had been new to the company in October 1964, and the Eastern Coach Works body provided comfortable seating for 60 passengers. Notice the flat lower saloon floor, the fluorescent lighting and the Cave-Browne-Cave heater outlets at ceiling level. BEL 679B was in service with Hants & Dorset almost until the end of crew operation, being withdrawn in June 1980. Crew operation on Hants & Dorset buses finally ended when the South Wessex-branded MAP network was introduced in the Poole and Bournemouth area from 30 November 1980 (see also page 45). *Neil Goodrich*

OLD BASING The Market Analysis Project (MAP) was devised by the National Bus Company as a means of identifying, area by area in special studies, bus networks that could be maintained at acceptable levels of fares. During 1978 MAP surveys had been carried out on all of Hants & Dorset's bus routes, the company being divided up into a number of study bus systems for this purpose. Within Hants & Dorset the first revised network to be introduced as a result of the MAP survey was at Basingstoke, where the new routes were branded as 'Venturebus'; this new network commenced operation from 2 September 1979. A surprising feature of this posed publicity photograph taken at Old Basing is the bus stop flag, which is of the traditional Wilts & Dorset pattern – by that time almost all of these had been replaced by modern corporate identity flags including a pictogram of a single-deck bus. The bus is Bristol VRT RJT 151R, which had been new to Hants & Dorset in January 1977. *Hants & Dorset*

POOLE BUS STATION Late in 1981 Hants & Dorset acquired a number of Bristol LH6L single-deck buses, which were around a year or so old, from the Bristol Omnibus Company. They replaced older Bristol LH saloons from the Hants & Dorset fleet, which were withdrawn from service as their first seven-year Certificates of Fitness expired. The ex-Bristol buses ran in National Bus Company leaf green livery for some time, as exemplified by YAE 520V, seen shortly after acquisition awaiting its next turn of duty at Poole bus station. It had entered traffic with Bristol in November 1979 and was acquired by Hants & Dorset in December 1981. Notice the South Wessex vinyl; this was the branding for the Poole and Bournemouth area bus network following the introduction of the MAP-designed network from 30 November 1980. *Brian Jackson*

BOURNEMOUTH BUS STATION Following the disastrous fire in July 1976, Hants & Dorset continued to use the largely undamaged office block until June 1981, when the company's Head Office was moved to the House of Travel in Oxford Road, Bournemouth. The former bus station was subsequently demolished, with work starting in October 1982. This photograph shows demolition in progress, and is taken from almost the same point as the photograph on page 31 showing the coach exit from the damaged building. The two-tier design of the former structure can be clearly seen. After demolition the site was used as a car park for many years; it is now the location of the bh2 complex. *Neil Goodrich*

FINALE This unusual vehicle was first seen on page 25 of this book as Bristol LH6L NLJ 516M. After its bodywork was badly damaged in an accident, it was given this new replica charabanc body that was designed and built in Hants & Dorset's own workshops at Barton Park in 1982. It was given fleet number 86 and the registration number TR 6147, both of which had been carried by a Leyland Lion single-deck bus that had been in service with Hants & Dorset from 1929 until 1939. A nice touch is the application of the Hants & Dorset fleet name in the pre-war style. During the autumn of 1982 it was announced that Hants & Dorset was to be broken up into four operating units (Wilts & Dorset, Hampshire Bus, Provincial, and Shamrock & Rambler), together with free-standing engineering and secretarial services units, with effect from 1 April 1983. From that date the name Hants & Dorset was no longer seen on the sides of buses, although the title survives at Hants & Dorset Trim, an excellent vehicle repair company based at Barton Park. *Hants & Dorset*

EXETER ROAD, BOURNEMOUTH We are very fortunate that a number of former Hants & Dorset buses have been saved by preservationists and continue to provide a reminder of that well-loved company. A particularly interesting example is KEL 405, which had entered service with Hants & Dorset in May 1950 carrying a 28-seat luxury coach body by Portsmouth Aviation. In 1960 the chassis of this vehicle was lengthened to 30 feet and its six-cylinder Gardner engine was replaced by a Bristol AVW unit; a new Eastern Coach Works single-deck bus body was fitted, and from June 1961 KEL 405 began a new lease of life as a driver-only-operated Bristol LL6B bus. Following withdrawal in 1969 it was used by a Scout troop in Godalming in the early 1970s, later passing into preservation. At the time of this photograph, taken on Sunday 18 June 2006, KEL 405 was owned by Mr Mike Smith and was taking part in a re-enactment of a Hants & Dorset route 7 journey from Bournemouth to Swanage, a trip it would have made many times during its final eight years with Hants & Dorset. *Chris Harris*

POOLE Bristol FS6G 5677 EL had been new to Hants & Dorset at Woolston depot in February 1961. It was in service with the company until 1977, then spent a further four years as a driver training vehicle. It was subsequently preserved and returned to its original condition, and was photographed in Poole on 10 July 2016 awaiting its next turn of duty while taking part in the running day arranged to mark the centenary of the founding of Hants & Dorset as Bournemouth & District Motor Services in 1916. Notice the plate carrying the original fleet number, 1450, with yellow figures on a black background, which were the colours used to denote a vehicle allocated to Woolston depot. Notice also the advertisement for Radio Luxembourg – remember listening to that on 208 metres medium wave? *The late Robin Woodcock*

POOLE Also taking part in the Hants & Dorset Centenary event on 10 July 2016 was Bristol FLF6G GLJ 748D. New to Hants & Dorset in June 1966, this bus spent much of its service with the company based at Poole depot, although it was transferred to Southampton before withdrawal in May 1980. Appropriately, during the running day this vehicle was used on a couple of journeys that recreated the Hants & Dorset route 1 between Poole and Bournemouth via Penn Hill; it was caught by the camera setting out for Bournemouth from Poole. *The late Robin Woodcock*

POOLE BUS STATION When new to Morebus in 2009, Scania N230UD/Optare Olympus HF09 FVT entered service in 'Purbeck Breezer' livery and spent six years being used mostly on the route between Poole and Swanage via Wareham. It was then repainted in the Hants & Dorset Tilling Green livery as part of the Centenary celebrations in 2016, and was photographed entering Poole bus station during the running day on 10 July. This was an excellent celebration by Morebus of the company's distinguished past heritage, and it is pleasing to note that HF09 FVT continues to carry Hants & Dorset livery at the time of writing (2020). *The late Robin Woodcock*

Index of Vehicle types and places

HANTS & DORSET

HANTS & DORSET

HANTS & DORSET